Welcome
Music
Business.

*you're

FU*KED!

by
Martin Atkins,
Author of Tour:Smart

Written by Martin Atkins

Layout & Design by Eric McNary

Illustrations by Ryan Lykken

Many thanks to The staff at Invisible Records, Chicago

Why all of the fuckeds in this first part?

Well, there are 101 ways to get fucked in this business – the more you are aware of – the better off you'll be. Right?

This is a very dangerous world and when you come un-stuck it isn't always just "aw shucks that was wild" it could be bankruptcy, loss of friendships, divorce, death, you might end up in a cover band.

So here it is:
If you **KNOW** that you're **FUCKED**
Then you're **NOT**
If you think that you're **NOT**
THEN YOU ARE!

Isn't that lovely? Iambic pentangle?

It's a little bit Disney, a little bit Tarantino....two conflicting ideas, the yin, the yang, two halves making a black hole battling it out in the tumble dryer with someones severed foot.

I can feel the vibrations, the waves of deer in the headlights panic from here – you KNOW I'm right, you KNOW you are fucked dontcha? But, it is human nature to try and bury your head in something – blaming, toxic workloads, cleavage – but, come up for air for a minute, let the storm clouds of deception disappear and you'll KNOW that I'm right. You're fucked fucked fucked fucked fucked fucked fucked fucked fucked so get used to it (for a while anyway).
EMBRACE IT!
Buy the shirt and get the fuck on with it.

Peace love respect

Martin Atkins
Chicago, ILLANNOYS
November 2010

I'm going to start this with a bit that I have in Tour:Smart called "always think of your parents before getting shagged." In most walks of life, most disciplines, neighborhoods, communities, cliques, and clubs there is a certain amount of common sense. If any of us were buying a car we'd most probably ask a respected

friend if he or she has heard anything about that brand: gas mileage, diesel vs. unleaded, one make over another, either looking for anecdotal salvation from an exploding car, or taking a more scientific route and checking a vehicle's history – whilst not a guarantee of getting the very best, safest car – then at the very least, avoiding the once submerged vehicle chopped in two, rebuilt with the aid of a few spot welds and a New Jersey phone booth.

All of the above or, if this is the Chinese version, everything to the right makes perfect sense. What happens in the music business, however, is that ALL common sense flies out the window.

It is not stupidity. There are too many smart people fucked up by their addiction to what they thought the music business should be.

It's partly to do with nine pairs of rose colored spectacles (the ones that precede the brown colored underpants) the hope that everything will be ok, and a desire to **NOT** rock the boat with a silly, Emperor's New Clothes type question.

So, with so many self-fuelling IDIOTS trying to sell you their new informational equivalent to a vacuum cleaner haircut. I want to very strongly suggest to you that you check 1-2-3 anyone who is going to have anything to do with your band, period. You don't have to **ASK** for a formal résumé or CV; after all, these people aren't renting an apartment from you or marrying your younger sister, they're **JUST GOING TO** fucking be involved in everything you do from now on you fucking moron!

Anyway, having said all of that, I should tell you what I have been up to for the last 30 years, but it's going to take up a lot of room so you can either go to the back of the book and read all about me there or go to my new website www.whogivesafuck.com to see the 3D version.

FUCKED!
by: yourself.

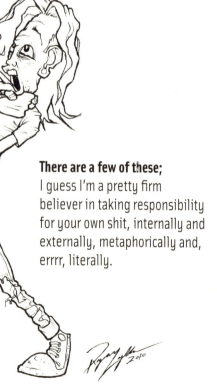

There are a few of these; I guess I'm a pretty firm believer in taking responsibility for your own shit, internally and externally, metaphorically and, errrr, literally.

#1 - Blaming

The music business is the easiest place in the world to blame someone – probably multiple people – **BUT** it's also a place where nobody cares and whatever words follow… 'It wasn't our fault…', 'If it wasn't for…', or ' We were fucked over by…' are as inaudible as a dog whistle to a heavy metal drum tech.

It's like the 'you had me at hello!' scene from Jerry McGuire, but you didn't have me at "It wasn't my fault" and, of course, no Tom Cruise.

Lame, right? So, once you understand that the only person paying for everyone else's lack of attention, stupidity, horrifying lack of a **CLUE** is **YOU** – your music, your career; then you'll understand that it is **YOU** that has to take 100% responsibility for everything that is going to happen with all of it – your music, your band, and your **BRAND**.

The good news is that **NONE** of this is rocket science. You can do large parts of it yourself, especially in the beginning **AND** as you move along you'll gain some of the additional knowledge and experience that you need, you'll also form a better idea of the qualities that you need in anyone that is going to help you – from sound to crew to manager or label.

So don't worry, you don't have to know how to negotiate a film-scoring gig with Steven Spielberg tomorrow – that will come in time… (the ability to negotiate – **NOT** the film scoring gig, dude – that's **NEVER** going to happen.) This is all stuff you can do!

FUCKED!
by: questionable advice.

Check the source or
you'll always
be playing *catch-up*.
HA!

Here are a couple of interesting quirky
anomalies, shall we say, that I've come
across recently...

Donald Passman

mentions in the introduction to his bible about the music business, that the most important creative decision a band will make is well, hang on, let's look at the other side of that question first. What is the reason that most bands break up? That would give us the answer to his question, right? The thing to be most avoided, the relevant, helpful piece of information from the master?

How many times have we turned on VH1 or flipped open a magazine to see another of our favorite bands bit the dust from musical differences (someone shagged the singer's girlfriend), drugs (someone shagged the singer's girlfriend and stole her drugs) or *actually*, shagging the singer's girlfriend.

Well, actually, **NO**, none of these. **Donald Passman** says the most important, creative decision your band will make is "choosing your attorney." **WHAAAAAT?** Are you fucking kidding me? Would you be shocked, astounded, and turn slightly green if I told you that **Donald Passman** is an attorney!?

We don't have to travel far to find our next source of really helpful information: **Mr. Ted Lathrop**. I was astounded and disappointed to see in the book he has on global marketing that one of the most important things you are going to want to check out before shopping an artist for foreign licensing (what is that anymore?) is the **"CIA's global corruption index."**

Surely knowing a person in a foreign country **OR** having less than 4 members in your band is **WAY** more of a determining factor of success?

There is so much terrific information out there, you just have to choose the people with the biases that you either understand, can see **OR** actually like and agree with. **IF** you think someone doesn't have a bias then keep looking – they do! I said the same thing in my book **Tour:Smart** available now on Amazon.com.

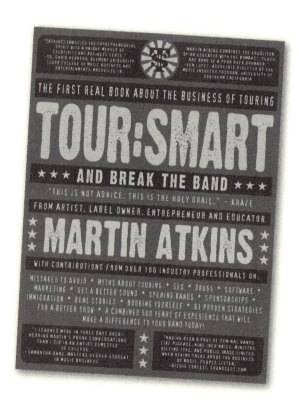

FUCKED!
by: yourself.

#2 - Ambition

This is a strange one. I'm not saying "don't have ambition." You **HAVE** to have it. But if your head is always looking up into the clouds or the twinkling stars (the celebrities, not the ones in space, silly!) you'll miss the next step which is just a little bit higher than the place you are standing right now.

If you are concerning yourself with the problem of how to put 20,000 people in a stadium…**YOU'RE FUCKED!**

I DON'T KNOW how you can put 20,000 people in a stadium,

but I know that if there were two people sitting on a couch in the corner of the room right now – you could make friends with them – or at least make contact, have a conversation- exchange your music, a CD, a shirt, a download card whatever for an e-mail address – and **BINGO!** – All you need to do is **THIS VERY THING** 9,998 more times and you have your 20,000 people!

File this one in the category: motivational poster. "It's not the destination; it's the free tickets to see Journey."

Of course this means that "people skills" must be packed in your new shiny diversified tool kit. Don't fool yourself. Not everyone is born with these skills. But, the more you practice the better you will become at anything. I'm very shy and look at me…sitting alone in a basement typing!

FUCKED!
by: lack of members of TEAM YOU!

How tragic is it, with all of the obstacles to overcome: finances shyness, geography, lack of time, technical stuff, workload that one of the largest obstacles to your success might be YOU?!

There's a reason

these behaviors are called self-destructive. You might think you are destroying a wall, another person's viewpoint, an argument, another bottle of vodka, but what you might be destroying is yourself!
Ouch.

I have seen this stuff so many times it's not funny anymore.
Be careful that your insecurities don't manifest themselves as some kind of raucous asshole-type behavior *because you think that's how rock stars act*. **Real stars are nice to people and connect with their fans** (that's all that's left, really).

The connection that you make with people is fragile. You can either help it along or destroy it.

You have to create a FACE TIME CONTINUUM!!

Unfortunately any opportunities (to fail or to shine) will be accompanied and multiplied by the x-factor, karma, and Murphy's Law.

Be the most valuable member of

FUCKED!
by: yourself.

#3 - The Pursuit of Purrrfection.

You don't need to make albums any more. Incremental releases of EPs or singles are much easier and more effective. You won't get completely clogged up with the mammoth task of creativity.

You need feedback from your audience (if you're smart).

How can you get feedback before something exists?

You can spend months tweaking a version of a song but let go, lighten up; nobody gives **two shits*** right now. Just release something – in small quantity. The sooner you start the earning and the learning, the better.

The *sooner* you release version 1.0, the *sooner* you can come out with version 2.0, version 3.0. Then, several years later, the miraculous overnight sensation version 4.0!

One way of thinking about the damage done by pursuing perfection might be helped if I tell you the...

Christmas Album Effect:

A mediocre Christmas album that's finished on Oct 25th is better than an amazing Christmas album finished on Jan 1st, right?

*Actually, nobody gives one.

FUCKED!
by: listening to someone else's fucked up agenda.

Be careful that you don't get pulled into someone else's trade war masquerading as a crusade. At least make sure that you Heinz 57 or litmus test the fuck out of any situation before you jump in...

* See Page 102

FUCKED!
by: the pursuit of technical ability.

If you're a drummer, maybe you'll want to be compared to Danny from TOOL, **YOUR CHOICES ARE:** give up (because none of us will ever be as good as Danny) or bring some other skill sets to the table: accounting, a little bit of Chinese translation, pancakes, vehicle maintenance? That could be you if you'd stop practicing your meaningless para-diddles.

If you don't believe me or think that this doesn't apply to you and your discipline, Just type "name of your field of expertise" + "child prodigy" into YouTube and stand back. Watch a bunch of five to nine year old children shred your ass...weep, cry yourself to sleep. Wake up and start working on more skills.

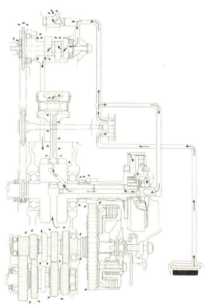

FUCKED!
by: conforming to someone else's idea of $ucce$$

You might want to

spend a little bit of quiet, alone time thinking about what success really means to you. **NOT** the cookie-cut and paste answer from 1,000 other interviews you've heard like, "a billboard #1" or "just being able to make a living making my music." Really think about it! There are all kinds of variants to the definition of success. Over my last year of travels, I've heard success variously defined as the two previously mentioned, as well as: 'getting signed,' (c'mon!) "drugs, world travel," and so wonderfully at a lecture in Manchester UK: "titties!"

Watch out for anything that is **EXTERNAL**. Success is like bad gas or appendicitis. It's internal.

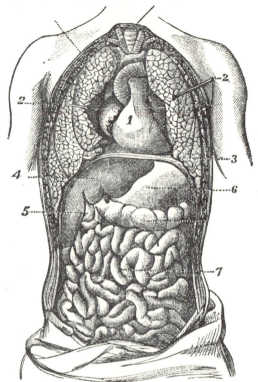

Fig. 14.

SUCCESS

FUCKED!
by: the law!

A CONTRACT IS NOT PROTECTION – EVER!

LEVERAGE IS!

You and your

attorney can come up with all kinds of neat paragraphs and penalties for non-completion of certain requirements - but **THE FACT is...**

If you don't sell any tickets – you're not getting paid.

You can point to the contract and talk about suing all you want, but are you really going to hire an attorney, sue, and then travel back to that god-forsaken town?

There is more progress to be made by positive motion forward, than by negative motion backwards! Also, you'll look silly banging around the room, waving your arms around, threatening a lawsuit.

Sell tickets and you can get whatever you want. Feel like drinking some Cristal, Black Label and eating sushi before your show? When you sell out a show you can get whatever the fuck you want.

Until then – shut UP!!

FUCKED!

by: yourself.
#4: the need for more external validation: Equipment & Sponsorships.

As artists,

many of us crave validation from the manufacturers of our favorite, most trusted instruments long after any real benefit of free gear has any financial meaning.

It's the check mark, the seal of approval and the carry over from our younger days spent sitting and staring through the window of the music store, the long hours spent looking in the pages of the magazines or staring at our favorite band with racks and racks of that very special equipment that makes the echo travel forwards in time.

You don't **need** an instrument endorsement! (Which is **GREAT NEWS because you're not going to get one until you don't need one.**) What you do need is relationships with more and more like-minded people…

It's really easy to start the relationship you want with the guitar company you worship – buy one.

FUCKED!
by: lack of a strategy.

Have a strategy! I know people who spend more time planning Thanksgiving dinner than their careers.

I love Sun Tzu's quote from the Art of War, **"never take your country to war unless you are sure of the outcome."** Well, let's change that to, "never take your band to perform in Cleveland unless you are sure some people will show up!" Actually, it should be, "never arbitrarily decide to take your band anywhere except where your fans already are and you have demonstrated that there are enough of them to start something (even if its just a hand of poker)." **OK?**

There are so many ways to track your fans. Bandcamp.com enables you to exchange free music in different quality formats for an e-mail address and the very, **VERY** important **ZIP CODE.** YouTube is now the second largest search engine and has amazing tools to help you look at your data geographically. TopSpin amalgamates many of the features that are out there into a new platform. The Orchard has their heat map. MySpace is frantically adding tools to help bands, and there's also Reverbnation.com, Nimbit, and add-ons from North Social and many, many more… **USE THEM.**

FUCKED!

by: not being on the cutting edge of the newest technological innovations.

This is a

double edged sword, "YES!" Stay on top of the newest innovations, platforms and tools (many of them are mentioned in the previous chapter), but don't be a slave to them. **USE the tools that work for you, don't let them use and consume you.** That's part of the new requirement of an artist: surfing on top of the shit-storm of innovations, using the ones that work for you to underline and reinforce your vision, not diluting it with pre-packaged templates that are in someone else's shrink-wrapped stackable voice.

FUCKED!
by: conformity.
do the opposite!

One of my strategies from ages ago is Do The Opposite or D.T.O. at first. I thought I might just be reinforcing my contrary, pissed off behaviour patterns, hiding behind a supposed marketing technique – but, I keep finding terrific examples of people who have simply done the opposite of what was expected was the norm – and have had amazing results.

Can't help but wonder what would have happened if the recording industry had D.T.O'd at the beginning of this whole downloading war debacle…don't they know? It's not a problem if 20,000 people have **'illegally'** downloaded your new album; it's a problem if they **HAVEN'T!**

- When EVERYONE is on the internet,
    Send a postcard!
- Looking for someone to promote your shiny new religion?
    Hire an atheist.
- Worried about heroin addiction?
    Give out free heroin!
- Want people to buy more cars?
    Give them stickers to keep the salespeople away.

If in doubt,

FUCKED!

by: by
exhaustion and
not knowing you
are exhausted.
(road lag)

THIS IS YOUR BRAIN

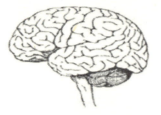

THIS IS YOUR BRAIN ON TOUR

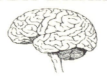

On a recent trip

to the West Coast, I think I did 12 events in 9 days. It was quite stressful. I could definitely feel the force fields at work: the tour manager's brain leaping ahead to find problems, opportunities for sleep, and constantly gauging the benefits of a free breakfast vs. another 60 minutes of sleep.

It wasn't until the last event was over that I relaxed: 'phew, I did it, danger is over!' Except it wasn't. I left my laptop bag in the parking lot of Cal Poly and lost my computer, cameras, green card, cash!

The danger of too-early-relaxation at the idea of a job well done, except it wasn't over yet.

I let my guard down and I was still 2,000 miles from home.

My Norwegian friend, Kjetil's band went to Mexico and were hyper vigilant. It was only when they arrived back at Oslo airport did they exhale, smile and get their gear stolen! It's not over 'til it's over.

FUCKED!
by: geography.

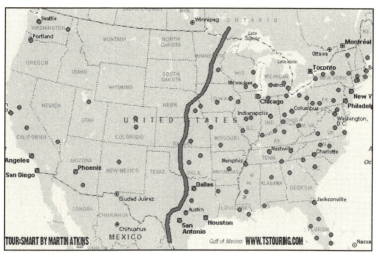

As I so fantastically said in Tour:Smart, America is **BIG**.... **REALLY** big! The distances, temperatures, terrain, and time will kill you, your vehicles and your dreams. It's difficult to keep up momentum when your van or your brain won't turn over. Stay East of that line.

There are more shows and less mileage expenses in a **WAY** smaller area. You'll have more time to socialize, meet new people, explore, market, fix your equipment and your brain.

FUCKED!
by: gas.

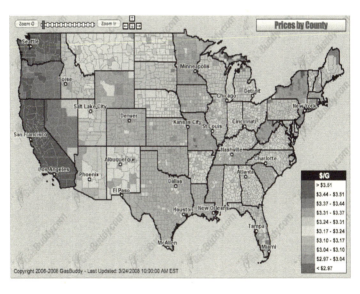

You'll be driving farther, faster out West, shredding your MPG and paying the most $ for gas! The combination of these factors **PLUS** the hours you'll be spending in the vehicle instead of interacting – or showering – make it a bad choice. There are great tips in Tour:Smart on how to get better live sound and how to be a better opening band, but one way to **REALLY** make a difference is to get to a show early.

One factor in

cementing the fragile bonds and memorializing the ethereal vibe you have (hopefully) created in the room you just performed in is by interacting with fans for an extended time after the show. Anything from exchanging e mail addresses to (very very carefully) bodily fluids, from listening to someone's opinions to listening to their all vinyl Bay City Rollers album collection at 3am and 33rpm. These are the shared experiences that will resonate through the years and hopefully decades to come. There's not much of that going on when you are already **LATE** for your next show 800 miles away.

FUCKED!
by: demographics.

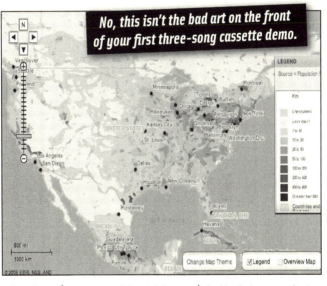

No, this isn't the bad art on the front of your first three-song cassette demo.

* Not really

Interesting fact: (courtesy of David Cooper) 60% of the population of North America lives within a one-hour plane flight from Philadelphia. One reason for you not bothering with the part of the country west of that line...**there's nobody there!***

If you live in California, you should buy the west coast version of this book. It's all the same great strategies, but all of the jokes are at the expense of the east coast instead.

FUCKED!
by: buying on to a show.

Buy on, tune up, and play well.
I'm not on the same page as many indie artists here. **The right buy on** can be beneficial for all. *The problem is finding the right one.*

As more bands look to monetize every available asset they have and more artists look to try and "leap frog" themselves a few rungs up the ladder by any means necessary, the 'buy on' (purchasing an opening slot with a more popular national touring band) has become quite common. Unfortunately, the rose colored spectacle phenomenon, simply not paying enough attention or inexperience, can lead to all kinds of problems.

Sometimes the main band can find themselves surprised and ambushed by low turn outs and shredded guarantees. These problems will be passed down the line to you. You might be expecting to play to 'sold out' shows but if attendance is bad, there's not really much you can do, except be very, very careful going in, there's no easy out.

FUCKED!
by: not being honest or real.

It's show business. The definition of honest is a little bit flexible, but as more and more of the traditional business disappears, there are some great thinkers and marketers who are now selling bags of hot flaming dog shit to eager artists.

If it appears to be too good to be true and much, much easier than doing the work of creating an audience and practicing your craft, it is! **You can't fill a room with smoke and mirrors.** Well, actually you can, it's called Studio 54, but you know what I mean.

As attractive as it might seem to jack up your fan numbers, it's going to become very obvious very quickly that these people don't exist when you play a live show! Do the work and earn your fans.

The only external validation you need is from your fans. Make sure that you don't pollute that feedback by adding meaningless, non-existent people to your social media platforms, or by buying into services that make your insecure self feel better about the number of fans you have.

Remember: if you haven't interacted with your fans in some way, they aren't really your fans.

FUCKED!
by: body odor.

It doesn't matter how fucking good you are on your instrument of choice if you have **ZERO** people skills, or lets say: **NO** personal hygiene, right? Let's keep it simple.

It doesn't matter how good of an engineer you are...
...if you STINK!

It doesn't matter

how good of a violinist you are if you cannot get up in the morning and catch a bus.

Pursuing technical ability on its own, for its own sake is a path to nowhere.

The beginning of punk was very simple; this quote is credited to Sniffin' Glue fanzine, but it was actually a 'zine called Sideburns:

'Here's a chord, here's another – now form a band!'

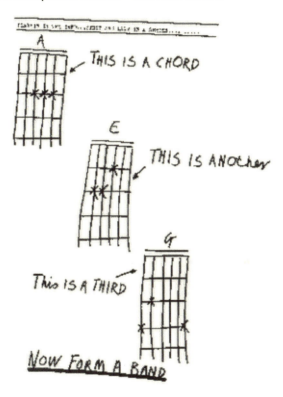

It's the other stuff you learn along the way that makes your career sustainable.

FUCKED!
by: choosing a venue that's too big!

Why is it that when bands are given the choice between a 500 capacity venue and a 900 capacity one, they choose the 1500 seat auditorium?

What's the worst thing that can happen if you choose a venue that's too small? **It'll SELL the fuck OUT!!**

Always choose a venue that's too small rather than too big!

FUCKED!
by: premature delegation.

This is very simple, if you don't know **YOUR** unique business **BEFORE** you head into this stuff, how can you possibly know the qualities you want in (say) an agent? Or the number and type of shows that work best for your band?? If you haven't done the research, (in the form of live shows) **how do you know what your most popular songs are?**

Sure you can look at your downloads and plays, but it's in front of a live audience that you can **FEEL** just how good a song is. Playing a song live is where you'll find out where it drags, where it works and where it doesn't. If the audience stands up and walks out - there's a hint for ya…

Push as hard as you can and learn as much as you can before you bring more people in to help.

FUCKED!
by: not doing it yourself.

do it yourself.

FUCKED!

by: hoping that people will do what you think they should or what they said they would.

This belongs in the 'fucked by yourself' category. There's really no such thing as a promoter anymore.

The best way forward for you is to **ASS**-ume that all a 'promoter' is going to do is open the doors of the venue... that's **IT**!

This way you can **NEVER** be disappointed! If you find someone that cares, be very very nice to that person. Promoters are not magicians; they open the doors to the venue and look at **YOU** when no-one shows up. They are **ASS**-uming that you have booked yourself into this too-large venue because you have been working your ass off to fill it.

This leads very nicely into:

FUCKED!

by: not knowing that nobody gives a shit about the things that are most important to you.

...except you

Nobody does! And, deep down, although you WANT to think otherwise, you KNOW that this is true! Cut this out and paste it on the rehearsal room door, or next to your computer.

FUCKED!
by: the need for external validation
- part two -
Record Deals

Why... to get signed.
I think the idea of wanting to sign to a label defines the gap between logical, objective thought and a more subjective process that is a large part of music and any endeavor that moves us. It's easy to look at some spreadsheets and show why it doesn't make any sense for one particular band or another to sign with a label. There used to be advantages in terms of the weight of the label's catalog, leverage, and great opportunities. Certainly in my labels' past we did tremendous and ridiculous amounts of work to help bands but you don't need a label anymore. You need alliances, a network, and some people to watch your back, but not a label.

Let's jump outside

of music business for a minute and consider the movie, In Bruges. The movie stars Colin Farrell as a hit man. After a botched job, his boss sends him to Bruges as a special treat to have a couple of enjoyable days before he is, in turn, shot. Part of the unfolding of the movie centers around the unfathomable choice of this city (or indeed any city in Belgium) as a place for someone to spend their last 48 hours. Once you've sent all of your friends the obligatory postcard of the pissing man fountain, that's pretty much it. I'm not slagging on Belgium but I think we can all agree that it is not really any kind of "cherry on top" of the lifetime cake. But, (and yes, here's the point I was trying to get to): for Colin Farrell's boss, Bruges held an idyllic meaning beyond the sum total of great  restaurants, opportunities for drugs, strip clubs, soccer teams, quality of beer, number of cable TV stations, divided by the benefits of the downside of a poor exchange rate.

  Bruges, to him, was a place where his father had spent time with him, bought an ice cream and paid attention. Special, revered, and mythical.

  And so, here we are. Even though the music business (on a good day) is an ornate fountain with a man pissing in it, there are still people for whom participation in it by way of being signed by a label is **the only way to be made whole, be confirmed or be recognized.**

 What a thrill to accidentally stumble across Belgium's true, most significant value as a metaphor for the shitty, still clinging to the bowl after two flushes, traditional music business.

FUCKED!

by:
manufacturing miniums that push you into manufacturing less designs and fewer versions in larger quantities

The first shirt

you design and order will be a shirt that doesn't sell very well in the wrong sizes and the wrong colors. You'll know as soon as you set it out on your merchandise booth that's it's **NEVER** going to sell, but you'll keep trying to sell it anyway. (That's natural) You paid for them and you should sell them all before you order more, right? **NO!**

 As soon as you realize it's a SHIT DESIGN that no one wants – ditch it! It pollutes the vibe of your merchandise booth, **AND** it traps you in the past. It doesn't matter how long ago it was that you realized it was a bad, poorly executed design. It makes no difference whether it was one week one year or one minute ago... it's time for version 2.0! **That's the value of the first bad shirt – using it as a learning platform for the next one.**

Practice this with your songs too!

FUCKED!
by: overplaying your local market.

Touring is tough and dangerous and maybe you haven't realized yet that you don't need an agent so you feel trapped in your city. You do what an awful lot of bands do – overplay your local market.

DON'T ask your friends if you are playing too much, **YOU ARE!** And it's their job to lie to you.

The easiest way to make your shows an event is to have them happen less frequently.

Only play when you have a new release or a new t-shirt design.

Get out of town, gig swap.

FUCKED!
by: not reading the fine print
and ASSuming!

I read a Facebook post from a local band that had a great show.

They generated $900 at the door and I'm sure a healthy ring at the bar.

The band only received $40. They didn't read the fine print.

Don't assume anything: number of guests, number of towels, number of other bands, anything.

FUCKED!
by: relying on anyone.

DO as much as you can yourself at first. It's not a problem that you don't know the main people at Rolling Stone magazine or Pitchfork.com (and a publicist won't solve that problem anyway.)

All ANYONE that is going to help you will do is **USE** the **BUILDING BLOCKS** that you have created yourself, and try to build something with them.

If you don't have **ANY** building blocks, there is a limit to what anyone can do to help you. There has to be a story of struggle so you can say, "Look what we did on our own without constant prodding and childlike supervision."

Then you can pose the question, "If you help us a little bit, how far could we go??"

Rely on yourself –
  at least you KNOW
how unreliable you are.

FUCKED!
by: choosing the wrong people to be in a band with.

It's not all about choosing the safest, most punctual, polite, tidiest band members with the best credit ratings and cleanest driving record. Those qualities don't make up a band that draws fans to the venue, do they? There's no risk, no danger, nor anything to compel fans to watch. I recently bought a shabby louvered door for my boys' room. I stripped it back, got rid of all of the caked-on flakiness from 50 years of built up paint. Hours later, I stood back to admire my work. I was patting myself on the back for a job well done when… the door crumbled and fell apart. It turned out that it was being held together by all of the shitty flaky paint. **Moral of the story – sometimes you need a bit of flakiness and some badass stripper!**

CHOOSE the drummer that shows up (if one does). Then, if you are struggling between two – choose the one with the smallest kit who doesn't want to change drum heads every day (ask them!) or the one that hears you when you ask if they can play a little quieter. Or choose the one with the ultra hot girlfriend.

CHOOSE the bass player with the van and the rehearsal space he built with the proceeds from the car accident settlement - unless he is totally shit and can't play bass. Then think about going all Human League and having him stand behind a keyboard with dark glasses and use a sequencer (and his van).

CHOOSE the guitarist that has several cup holders already built into his equipment along with ashtrays and several cigarette lighters Velcro-ed to his amp along with a blender. This is the mark of a true professional – you are in the presence of greatness.

CHOOSE wisely, surprisingly, and understand the consequences – one of them being that if you follow all of the rules of business and just choose two other people to be in your band based upon their assets instead of choosing the five nut jobs you really want to be in a band with then you might be fucked before you start. But you'll have a hell of a time not getting there.

Get some balance so that you can be totally unbalanced in a deliberate way.

Understand that chemistry is unfathomable to stage, direct or plan for. There isn't a recipe for this stuff, well there kind of is.
Sometimes it's the opposite of a recipe. Sometimes it's some of the same ingredients put together in a different order, half baked or crispy around the edges.

FUCKED!
by: fractured rights.

You don't need a deal with anyone anymore. Hold on to all of your rights to everything. Read about the band Metric. They spent time and money reacquiring rights that had been sold before setting out to conquer the world.

When you control all of your rights, all of your decisions can be made quickly. You can give away a t-shirt because it only cost you $1.50 to make (and you have the rights). You can let a company do something with the stems from your multi-tracks **because you control them.** You can give someone CDs or download codes (because you have the rights). You can agree to give a young filmmaker some songs (because you have the rights).

In the world we are in NOW it will take too much time to get permission from all of the other rights holders and will ruin any opportunities. You need to be able to respond to an opportunity quickly and in the moment – not three weeks later when your rights-holders get back to you.

You need to be able to say YES to anything in a heartbeat.

FUCKED!
by: not always asking why!

(Taken from Tour:Smart)

WHY – are you heading west?
WHY – did you choose this agent?
WHY – didn't you book this yourself?
WHY – did the ticket price get that high? Are you worth it? Would you pay that much to see you?
WHY – is it time to make another album, how many has the last one sold?

FUCKED!
by: valuing $$ more than relationships.

The surest way to destroy something is by pursuing money. Pursue and fuel relationships and, eventually, you will have $$$. Pursue $$ and you will get nothing.

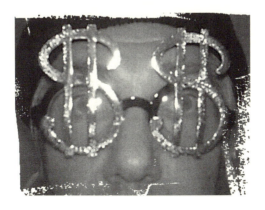

FUCKED!
by: not listening, or by listening too much.

Part of this is knowing when to open up, listen, and digest all of the information that is available to you. But (here's the tricky part) once you have done this…

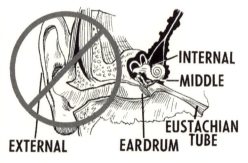

…you need to put your helmet back on, turn on the noise-cancelling headphones, put on the welding goggles, and get on with it. Don't worry! You'll find the sweet spot at the intersection of attention and ignorance after a while.

FUCKED!
by: being anal.

Thinking you need to finish one task before you start another. Spin those plates! Sometimes you can get great traction by promoting one event with another... before one task is over and the other has begun.

FUCKED!
by: your gear fetish.

A hopeless addiction to analog gear or software or hardware or...

FUCKED!
by: laziness.

...in body and brain.

Henry Ford said, "Whether you think you can or you think you can't, both of those things are true." Start now! Look out for fear masquerading as uber-cool laziness. It's not, it's fear! The only thing to fear is beer itself.

FUCKED!
by: thinking it's cool not to know how to use Excel.

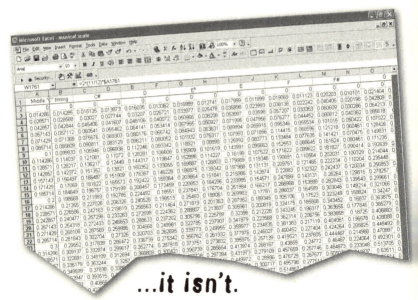

...it isn't.

And it's way easier than you think.

FUCKED!
by: by thinking it's 1980

...either in the record label advance department or in the transaction department. Back in 1980 you sold something for money – a simple one-ply transaction. Now there are tears, anxiety, and a three-ply Kleenex before the transaction is complete.

FUCKED!
by: not having a range of merchandise for sale

You need your album – or, if you haven't mastered it yet - split it up into three or four EPs.
- You need your other albums
- You need a live album for every gig you've done
- Release the demos, only people that like you will get them. They might never listen to them really, and if they do, they have already decided they like you and your songs. So relax, they won't be listening and thinking, "oh my God – this sounds like a demo;" **IT IS A DEMO**. And the C60 memory cassette of the song will be playing in their head when they listen.

  Give fans the stems so that they can mix their own shitty versions for themselves and *their* friends.
- Pretend to go to Germany and record a live album.
- Get a flip cam and throw together some short bits for YouTube. Put them all together onto a DVD.

Make your own merchandise – shirts, sweat shirts, sweat pants, workshirts, bags, wrist bands, head bands, hats, bejeweled scarve thingies that people complain about because they are scratchy. Stop making those and bejewel something else, like pants, underwear or coffee mugs. Be careful because they break; make posters, banners, anything and everything in small quantities at first (good job you only made three of the scratchy scarves, right?)

FUCKED!
by: treating your social media like a megaphone

...it isn't.

FUCKED!
by: a chicken burrito.

Pay attention to food choices on the road!
From Chipotle:
The Chicken Burrito bowl is 489 calories! The chicken burrito is 1092! That's a difference of 603 calories!

Just like an ill-advised reunion show or late night activity of any kind, a bad meal once in a while doesn't do too much harm, but, if you're intending to spend any amount of time on the road, then these decisions will start to add up. With a little bit of knowledge a few simple decisions can start to make an incremental difference in your outlook and your health. Just imagine what might have happened if you'd used the same effort choosing your bass player!

FUCKED!
by: waiting to jump in.

The longer you wait, the further behind you'll be. If you start waiting for the next version of the software, the update, the right time, the bugs to be worked out, the price to decrease, you'll be so far behind the curve it'll be like making a new album on 8 track tape, oh, hang on… Let's change this to: either stay remotely in the slip stream ahead of the curve (within 12 months or so), just long enough for the price to come down and all kinds of amazing shit to be on craigslist as they early adapters dump their ridiculously funny antique 12 month-old shit…or, stay so far behind the curve that you are amazingly surfing on the top of the renaissance. **It's like staying up so late that you're first one down to breakfast.**

FUCKED!
by: karma.

We can look at it the other way and fold Murphy's Law (not James Murphy from LCD Soundsystem, the other one) into this.

 The person that you are nasty to today will be in a position to make your life miserable at some point in the future and by some karmic multiple of your action. It might be a parking ticket, a small decision that really messes with you ("I'm sorry sir, the restaurant is full this Valentine's Day evening") or it could have tenfold impact from someone in the role of gatekeeper, a velvet rope doorman between you and the VIP room but, mark my words – **it will come to pass and bite you in the ass!**

UN
FUCKED!

"out of the virus,
immunity comes..."
- Killing Joke

Make a flyer and give it out:
The main purpose of flyering is to give yourself a reason to hang out on the street, stop people, **REAL PEOPLE** and talk to them! The flyer isn't the end result; it is the excuse for a conversation that leads to a relationship. **Pheromones not telephones!**

Don't Overplay your Local Market:

Make your show an **EVENT!** The simple rule of thumb is playing every 9 to 12 weeks **OR** whenever you have a new t-shirt design. Don't ask your friends if playing every two weeks is too much. They are your friends – it's their job to lie to you and they will!

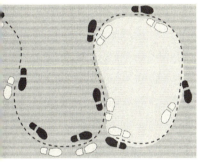

Expand your gig base carefully.

Be like the coyote on a frozen lake. You don't jump from one position to the next; you very gingerly test the ice with one foot, balancing your weight on the other. Once you **KNOW** that the ice is firm, then you transfer your weight to your other foot.
DO EXACTLY THAT but with gigs in markets outside your home city and very, very carefully.

UNFUCKED!

Use the Five Pointed Star Inward Facing Crush Technique:

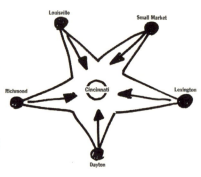

I understand that you want and NEED to perform more than once every 9 to 12 weeks. So, start to travel in a 50 mile radius. Find out of the way places to build your audience instead of playing the same club over and over and over to fewer and fewer people.

Think of yourself as a Drug Dealer - Play for Free:

The first few hits are free and as long as you have good shit, the people will come, and come back for more. Just remember not to sprinkle too much baby laxative on your product.

 Ask yourself, how much you would pay to see you? How many of your friends have any money? **EXACTLY!** It makes your show immediately more attractive than many of the others that week. People will have more money for beer and merchandise. You're not giving anything away, really. You're just pulling in more people to be randomly **EXPOSED TO YOUR** amazing **ARTISTRY** and become addicted to you **FOR LIFE.**

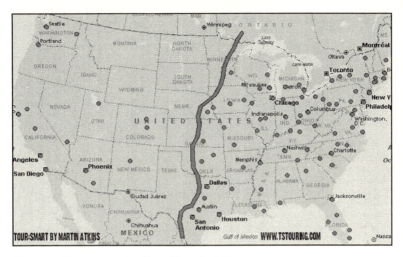

Tour East of the Red Line:

My favorite map of all time shows how important looking at information in a clear way can be such a massive help! (Or could have been if I'd taken the time to do this map 20 years ago.) These are the top 100 largest markets across the US:

Don't go west of that red line – When you factor in the mileage, wear and tear on your vehicle and your brains, along with the danger of long drives and bad road conditions, (in the summer across the deserts and the winter across the mountains) it makes it a really sensible strategy to stay **EAST**. That **DOESN'T** mean: 'Lets move to New York City!" I didn't say that, and in fact that will kill you too. (Maybe think about Nashville, Louisville, or Chicago.)

Book Yourself:

We've established that no one cares more than you. Only **YOU** can make decisions about playing the **RIGHT** venue for free because it's a great long term career move. It's very difficult for an agent to do that! When you head out on tour, play, perform, or do something 11 times a week. (Yes, that means Saturday and Sunday afternoons, BUSKING in the car park, someone's basement, a train, a coffee shop, outside a sold out show). The more small steps you take, the quicker you'll get to wherever the fuck you are destined to be! And real people in venues like to have real relationships with artists (as long as you're not a pretentious insecure dick).

GET THE FUCK OUT OF BED!
Before you hire someone you don't really know to help you – **help yourself!** A few extra hours every morning or late at night (unless you are a drunken fuck-head) start to add up pretty quickly. An extra five hours a day equals 35 hours a week OR **140 hours a month** of special, quiet, and productive time.
New Rule: If you're not in bed by 10pm.... Go home!

Aim Low, Get High:
I was lucky enough to be at the Great Wall of China in 2006. It is a great metaphor for success, whatever that is. On the one hand, you can step back, look at the whole thing and scratch your head marveling at it's amazing-ness, muttering phrases like, "how did they do it?", "It's amazing", and "Phew" or you can realize that it's **just a fucking pile of bricks!** YES! It's an amazingly huge pile of amazingly old bricks but it is just a pile of bricks. Stop standing back, scratching your head marveling at somebody else's great wall and start your own!

Vidal Sassoon the fuck out of it
Find an action that works and repeat, rinse, repeat, rinse, repeat...

Perform, don't play:
Stop gazing at your shoes.
Put on a show. People go to see a show, not to *hear* a show. Watch a video of your performance and do more of the good stuff and less of the silly stuff. (Unless the silly stuff is amazing silly stuff then ignore my advice.) Play songs people want to hear not just your newest ones. The audience won't know them, yet, and they might not like them. Just because the songs are new to you doesn't mean jack. Familiarity is important.

You are working for the audience, not the other way around.

Practice for Catastrophe:

It's not about being able to put on a great performance when everything is perfect (monitors, underwear, quantity of whisky, stage height, lights, PA system, dressing room, availability of toilets, crowd response etc). **It's about being amazing when you absolutely shouldn't** and any self respecting spoiled artist would have thrown down their instruments and stormed off stage in a huff. Practice at being great in impossible situations. Laugh in the face of adversity, practice in three inches of water with only four strings on your guitar, piss dripping on your head, being electrocuted by faulty wiring and the microphone cutting in and out while the drummer is angrily throwing lit cigarettes in to your backpack which contains charcoal and lighter fluid in the event of an impromptu barbeque. Give yourself electric cattle prod shocks every time you gaze at your shoes and smile, smile, smile. When all of this happens at your opening slot at Lollapalooza, or (insert name of really important show here), you'll be amazing, overcome adversity and triumph. you've practiced for this... except for the horrifying attack of diarrhrea.

Because that's EVERY gig you'll ever play

The last thing you need is a plush, luxurious rehearsal space with reliable equipment.

Free is the New Black:

Be prepared to give away anything or **EVERYTHING** that you have made; not all of it all the time to one person, but whatever a person wants – **give it to them.**

Sell more than your studio album or EP. Sell a live album, remixes, demos, b-sides, whatever. **Give away your most precious item, your most expensive, or newest coolest shiniest object.** People will buy something else once you have shown them how much you like them. Exchange your stuff for email addresses. (There are many elegant tools to help you do this.)

If in doubt, **think like a bakery.** Should you give away your best, nicest, most expensive and time consuming to make cookie? Or the leftover, stale, not very popular bagel chips from late last week? **RISE above and...get the dough!** After all, you're not giving someone a gift. You're handing them an exploding **GUILT BOMB!!**

You can research great examples of FITNB with:
- Monty Phython- 23,000% increase in revenue
- Prince- Millions made from 20+ sold out shows at London's O2 Arena
- Panera- Giving away free food!
- Radiohead- Choose your price album sales

Make Cool Shit:

Make your work VIBRATE with your unique energy and your creative DNA. There are so many benefits to unique packaging. It makes you stand out from the competition, it's a great exercise for your band to think more clearly about what it is that you are (heavy, shiny, soft and furry, cuddly, nasty, rusty, etc). Make sure that the answer to the question, "Do I want to open this package and check out what's inside?" is **YES!**

Unique packaging has always made an impression on me, I played on PiL's Metal Box in 1979. Three 12" singles in a film cannister. I've seen the value, the longevity that the extra effort can give back.
Only a couple of years ago the Wall Street Journal ran a piece about the album, 30 years after it was released.

Great packaging won't save a shitty, badly-recorded album but when it is combined with a great album it creates the kind of wrong math that I love.

1 + 1 = 11!

Another great example is Moldover. His album is a traditional CD with the backing made out of a circuit board. The song titles are written in circuitry and a few electronic components make a light sensitive Theramin complete with a headphone out jack! The time, effort and imagination put into this have paid off many times over. I've spent the last 12 months travelling the world and at every

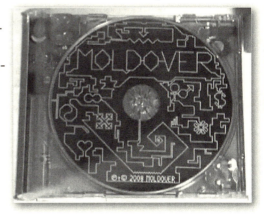

opportunity I evangelize about this amazing guy and his album. I'm not his manager, agent, label or publicist but I'm always talking about his amazing shit! Same goes for Kimberly Freeman and One Eyed Doll – the story of her evolution is inspiring.

Your imagination is a powerful tool – use it.

Use Free Tools & the Internet; find out where your fans are and play there:

It's easier to deal with problems of equipment, staging, or no dressing room than it is to be well taken care of, but to have the problem of no one buying a ticket (We like Reverb Nation's Fan 360, Google Analytics, The Orchard's Heat map and YouTube Insight.) **Pay for stuff that you can't live without.** We are using Eventric's Master Tour at the office to help make sense of the insane amount of our events that are happening around the world.

Monetize the Space Around the Thing You Used to Sell

Get over the boring concept of trying to sell music! BMW runs an ad campaign with the slogan, "we sell **JOY!**" What is your band/brand selling? If your answer is nothing then you just don't get it and you won't get any. Don't let a German car company beat your ass in the groovy-ness conceptual turn around Olympics. Think, create, accumulate, stimulate!

Create a need and fill it. Someone just bought a virtual donkey on Farmville...the world is moving very fast. You can't spend any more time bleating about the way things used to be. Sell the space around the thing we used to sell; we say it was albums but I think it was always **VIBE.** And when someone comes up to your merch booth that has already bought **EVERYTHING**, then make something up! Create a recipe book, sell that or give it away free and insert hard to find ingredients into the recipes and make those available on your website.

Fuck art and music - become a saffron dealer! They call me mellow yellow.

Stop Pursuing Perfection:

Don't worry if it isn't perfect, you don't even know what your audience wants yet. Be flexible and learn how to be **YOU.** Release singles, EPs, anything. You can always tweak the next version, EP 2.0. Eventually, you can compile the best into your first album. **THINGS CAN STAY FLUID AS YOU LEARN MORE ABOUT YOURSELVES, YOUR MUSIC, AND YOUR AUDIENCE.**

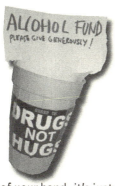

Have a Tip Jar with a Hilarious Message:

Make people laugh and give them a reason to put 25 cents or a dollar in your tip jar. Soon it'll add up and can fill your gas tank, your tummy or, if in fact you are a drug-addled idiot, your nose.

Once again, this isn't about one massive difference to the overall financial profile of your band, it's just **ANOTHER** 10 to 20 bucks a day coming in, not going out!

Have more than one of everything (t-Shirts, CDs, etc.):

Should the question be, "would you like to buy this shirt?" OR "WHICH of these two shirts would you like to buy... this one or that one?" The second is a VERY different question! *It doesn't include the answer "NO"* and it will make a HUGE difference to your tour as well as your ability to grow. This is NOT about how much money you can make from merchandise sales. It is about memorializing the fragile vibe that you have created in the room that night and sustaining it until you can return! By offering a choice you might sell five more shirts each night. After 100 shows there will be 500 more people wearing your shit! It's not about the money, it's about 500 people wearing your shirt.

Learn to Screen Print:

Not only does this skill allow you to express yourself and experiment in more ways, it removes the filters and time between more and better designs while underlining the unique qualities of your band. You can make merchandise so cheaply that you **WILL** be able to **GIVE IT AWAY** and create more new fans for next time. Then, make more of the stuff that sells and none of the stuff that doesn't!

You'll also be able to print a variety of products specifically suited to **YOUR** audience. You can manufacture in smaller quantities. Then, when you've sold five or ten you can put a sign up that says "new design – sold-out!" People will freak out, ask you if you have any hidden in the van, ask if they can buy the display model because now they **KNOW** it's a super cool shirt that everyone wants. You just made the shirt way more desirable. In fact, fuck it. Show up to your next gig with signs that say, "Sorry. New design **SOLD OUT!!**" Take orders, sizes and email addresses.

Mmmmmmm wake up and smell the plastisol!

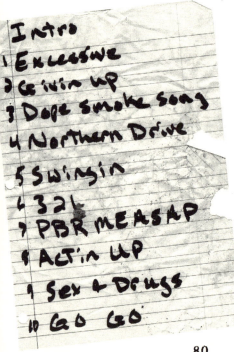

If the Lyrics of the Chorus Don't Belong on a T-Shirt...

...then maybe they don't belong in the chorus of your song??

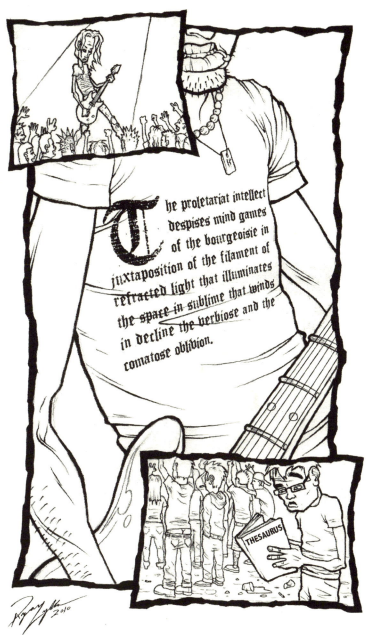

Build Relationships – Don't Acquire Customers:

These days, people are more interested in creating a relationship with you than buying your stuff. Eventually, the reason they will buy your stuff is because they feel connected to you. Your job is to facilitate these connections.

It has never been easier to find the people your music connects with.

Build bridges! It doesn't matter what direction the bridge is built. Once the bridge is built, it will work in both directions!!

The Golden Nugget:
My Book Tour:Smart:

There are 500+ pages of really great shit and its only $20 on Amazon. It's full of great stuff that will help and it's great to hit the drummer with or stop your van from rolling downhill in San Francisco. You can also *pre-order* my new book, **Band:Smart** due out in 2011.

Small is the New Huge:

Always choose the smaller venue. Two hundred people in a room that holds 750 is a catastrophe. Put those same people in a 150 capacity bar and it's a riot!

Never take your Country to War unless you're sure of the Outcome:

I said this earlier but I'm going to say it again and again.

Touring is warfare. Use your head and any information that is available to you to strategize where you are going to go. In fact, you shouldn't make this decision. Your *information* should dictate it to you. Find out where your fans are. You can press the "insight" button on your YouTube account. You can upload free songs or a digital mix tape and use any one of the amazing free tools that are out there to find out where your fans are.

Big Fish. Small Pond.
New York, Los Angeles, London, etc. will chew you up and spit you out. This is mentioned in Tour:Smart as **move to Boise!** **Start** somewhere small and become amazing there. **Then** take your success, your contacts and your experience and go somewhere larger. **Brick by brick by tick by tock.**

Don't give up and don't get discouraged.
If you find yourself giving up then start again, never stop. Persistence trumps talent. **ALWAYS.**

It takes years to build something amazing. Just keep getting up, and getting up, and getting up.

A Word on Social Media; Practice Japanese Table Manners:

No-one cares about ANYTHING anymore. The upside? They will happily tell you about the things they are interested in on their Facebook pages, LinkedIn profiles, Myspace Pages, etc – cars, guns, drugs, girls, gambling, organic food, circuit bending, fishing, ice hockey, ice fishing, ice ice baby, eagles (the birds not the band) tits! (the birds not the body part) cocks (ditto) swallows (ok stop!)

Form the bond first. You need more skills than just being good on your chosen instrument, you'll need social skills too. If you think you are too shy, overcome your shyness. Exercise that muscle just like you would practice your ultra fast fingering technique (and don't forget the guitar either!). "You can make more friends in two months by becoming

interested in other people than you can in two years by trying to get other people interested in you." – Dale Carnegie
Thanks, Dad.

Nobody cares, nobody cares, and nobody gives a fuck!

That's what the guys at Jagoff will take delight in telling you. If you are using social media to try and get people to your show **- STOP -** why would they come? They don't know you; they don't care. People will come and see you perform if they know you and like you even if they don't like the music. If they don't like you, you're fucked. In Japan, it is considered rude for a guest to pour his or her own drink – so everyone pays extra special attention to their guests – it's the only way to get them to realize your glass is empty and reciprocate.

Japanese Drinking Rules*
- **When drinking alcoholic beverages, it is customary to serve each other, rather than pouring your own beverage.**
- **Periodically check your friends' cups and refill their drinks if their cups are getting empty.**
- **Likewise, if someone wants to serve you more alcohol, you should quickly empty your glass and hold it towards that person.**

How to Make Your Show an Event:
(Excerpt from my Eventric Blog)

It's all well and good for all of us to keep shouting, "Make your show an event! Give people a REASON to come!" But maybe your head is so full from trying to make everything else happen that you can't come up with any ideas.

Here are a few bits and pieces to help get you started. There's more on my blog.

Start simple.
Use a landmark event in your band's history.
A CD release party is an event. Create more of them by releasing singles and EPs rather than a traditional album. You'll get four release events over a 12 month period.

Add a Cause.
It changes the question you're asking. Instead of, "Do you want to come see my band?" (Answer: No, I don't), you ask, "Do you want to help starving children in India?" You increase the chances of a better outcome for all concerned. This also gives you a reason to send out a legitimate update to everyone after the event. "Congratulations to all of us! We raised $500." BTW, you're also helping starving children in India.

Anything to do with firefighters or the police has a triple benefit of:
- charitable component
- increased likelihood of getting out of a speeding ticket ("Officer, we just performed a charity concert for the fraternal order of police")
- those guys have all the best drugs

Apply the 'get in free if...' model.

Offer the opportunity to "get in free" if a specific action is followed. This can be anything from frivolous crap to community outreach.

Assign a theme to the whole night.

You've been to 70s night at the ballpark, right? The White Sox biggest event! Yes, people look ridiculous, but it gives you and your audience something to talk about.

Hi-jack an event (piggyback).

Find a HUGE successful show that you have nothing to do with and..... **after party the fuck out of it!** The hardest thing to accomplish these days is getting people off the couch and out the door. With an event hi-jack, someone else has done the heavy lifting for you.

LIVE ALBUMS LET GO!!

It's not about the band, it's about the fan.

It is the sum of the fan's moments that resonate for them, the waves of energy that surround a point in time that sweeten the harsh tones of a bad recording, reduce the feedback and carry them along on a different journey more than a quantitative checklist of tone, tune and rendition. In this context the live album isn't a yardstick of sound quality or even adrenalized performance; it is simply a memory prompt. A stick in the dirt to remind us where the daffodils are.

Let's take a couple who met not on the night The Who recorded Live at Leeds, but two nights later at the Manchester show. For them, a shitty cassette that the husband surreptitiously recorded on a Radio Shack portable with a crappy stereo mic is ten times more important **TO THEM** than the hi-fidelity version of the Leeds performance.

So what does all of this mean to your bottom line and the sustainability of your brand?

THE SPIRITUAL SIDE

Stop gate-keeping concerts, supervising vibe and rationing moments. Any one of them could be very important to someone and ridiculously inconsequential to another. To think that the determining factor of a live album's success is the quality of the recordings is ridiculous. Fans have an internal sliding scale that excuses poor quality in direct proportion to the importance of everything surrounding the event. Has anyone ever criticized the graininess of the JFK assassination film or the glitchy-ness of the footage of the bomb going down the chimney in Iraq?

THE ECONOMICS

If you are serious about performing/breaking/sustaining or just being a great band and winning a larger audience, then you must perform 100 shows a year and maybe many many more. If you get into the habit of recording and making them available, the tide begins to turn in your favor.

If you have an audience of 100 people a night on average then you might sell 10 copies of that night's performance.

10 CDs x $5 = $50 a show – **that's your gas money!**

Playing 100 shows a year; you're looking at 1,000 CDs (or "units") in the next 365 days! In dollars and cents that's:

10 CDs x $5 x 100 shows = $5,000 a year – **that's your own van!!**

Who wouldn't want to sell that many live albums?

Give, Get, Make:

(Thoughts on how you are going to get paid.)

Wake up and smell the coolant in your overheating van. You are going to need to **be prepared to get paid – three times removed.**

"What's he talking about now?" you say. It's simple:

It used to be that we did something and we got paid for it. It used to be pretty straightforward…

- **Sell a t-shirt**
- **Make money**
- **GIVE** music to a TV show because it's a GREAT opportunity and you need the exposure!
- **GET** offered the tour that goes along with it; no payment but great exposure
- **MAKE** money on the t-shirts as the tour will be packed!!!

OR

GIVE shirts away at a free concert

GET e-mail addresses in exchange

MAKE money *next time* you play by incentivizing your new friends to come to the show and buy a new shirt.

GIVE GET MAKE requires you to be in control of your rights. Consider what you're really giving up when signing any contract. Look into the issue or fractured rights and refer to the example of the band Metric.

This concept is definitely in the Free Is The New Black family. Don't be frightened. I'm not saying everything has to be free and everything has to be given but when you have a product range (let's say five different physical releases) you can give one away and it will precipitate the purchase of another. If you only have one CD to give away or sell, then yes, you've nailed this one…you're totally fucked.

Not My Job!

I want this to be the last time that any of you thinks about the above sentence.

WHY? We all want a job description, right? And once we have one we then **KNOW** what our job is, right? Well, actually, no.

In my world (the world of self employed entrepreneurial multiple business plate spinning) there is no such thing as a comprehensive job description. I could very easily say that I was in this band or founded that band or that I made an award winning documentary or blah blah blah (and I just did). **BUT** that didn't make much difference to the stray, feral cats that started breeding in the gap between my Chicago studio and the neighbor's house.

So... while our interns were doing cool hipster social media marketing stuff, working on a sound library for our publishing company in the studio and updating the record label website, I was in the back alley being scratched by a cat wondering how my drumming was going to sound after my infected fingers were removed.

In my world, there is no such thing as "not my job" and anyone who says that in my building, in my presence, or in my studio can fuck the fuck off!

Fart in the Elevator:
The World Wide Web makes us tingle and widens our nostrils in anticipation of conquering the world- **NOT** going to happen. All you need to do is think locally. We're not looking for an action that will be felt around the world, but something that will make an indellible impression, a fart in an elevator. An event that will forever brand itself in the minds of the unlucky recipients who will always take the stairs from now on and tell the story... **STINK LOCALLY!**

Pour gasoline on the sparks...

...wherever they are. **START A FIRE.** When you arbitrarily decide where the sparks should be and pour your precious gasoline there, you're ignoring where the sparks actually are. The sparks will slowly fade, burn out, someone will slip and fall in the pool of gasoline, and sue you. Create a fire, create momentum. **MOMENTUM is key!** When you have momentum you can get $$ and the other things you want. When you only have money it's difficult and very dangerous to try and exchange that for momentum.

Commit...Risk

"You have to jump off the high dive board before the pool below is full of water." – *Gary Witt, Pabst Theater, Milwaukee.*

 Playing safe is the riskiest thing you can do.

On having great ideas...

It's not about trying to have the most amazing ideas and straining over the creative bowl for them to emerge fully-formed. Sometimes it's just about being a flower, opening up and absorbing as much of it all as you can. The creative process is crawling on the floor, eating all of the different colors of play-doh that you can then waiting, digesting, putting that stuff through your own internal filters and eventually seeing what kind of multicolored poop comes out the other end.

Open, absorb, shit it out.

Being good at one thing isn't enough anymore.

The phrase "jack of all trades, master of none" is from a different century and a different mindset. They told us A.D.D./A.D.H.D. was bad. Are you kidding me? It's exactly what you need to survive in the plate spinning, ever changing, entrepreneurial, multi-tasking world we are now in.

Add a skill to any other thing that you do:

Engineer
A new language
Hair styling
Childcare
Sewing
Screen printing
Web Design
Movie shooting and editing
Blogging
Vehicle maintenance
Dealing with the public
Modeling
Welding
Photography
Data
Computer Repair/networking
Latex crafting
Papermaking
Chef
Driver
Management
Accounting

You'll be more employable and, as budgets shrink and two jobs are combined into one to save money, bunks, air and space, you'll be able to step in, step up, and step lively!

There are no shortcuts.
No Economies of scale. It's just 27 hours a day, nine days a week, and 385 days a minute. The accountants can't make sense of the things that make a difference in art and culture based human interaction, but you can. The benefit is more than the value of the gift and the return you'll eventually receive. It's many times the value of that.

Teach yourself to use iMovie.
Get a flip cam and communicate in as many forums and mediums as you can. How many fishing lines do you want in the water, one or fifty? iMovie is super easy to use, and as effective as you need without chewing up loads of time.

Not how, what
It's not how you communicate, it's what! Twitter is the new fax. Don't be distracted by the new shiny object.

Be a speedboat, not an oil tanker.
It takes an oil tanker so long to change course that by the time it gets to where it decided to go, the reason it wanted to go there has disappeared. You need to be a speedboat. That's what I told Guy Hands' assistant three years ago.

Make 3D Decisions.
…data driven decisions. Look at any and all available data, then make decisions and plans based on that. Just gathering information, laying it out and looking at it can make a huge difference. It wasn't until I had the birth dates of my four boys tattooed on my arm that I realized three of them were born in July. I mean, obviously I knew that, I was there (except for Harrison, who was born prematurely in the UK) but it wasn't until looking at the data that it was obvious. Then, someone else said, what was happening every October? See, it's only once you lay out the data that you can analyze it.

Stop waiting…START!
I know you want to wait for the water to be warmer and experience less shrinkage when you jump in or you want to get everything just right for the arrival of your baby before you try and conceive, but you're going to wait an awful long time and the truth is **you'll never be ready.** Never for the stuff that's coming. The more you commit to in advance, the less flexible you'll be, and you need to be flexible.

You will amaze yourself with your abilities under pressure. You will be able to lift the equivalent of a car's worth of difficulties, bad reviews, negativities and set back from on top of the crying, puking baby of your body of work. You will move mountains and be totally amazing and inspiring to others but not while you're sketching it all out. There is stuff that you can't plan for, and that's that. You can prepare mind, body and spirit and have an extra print cartridge for your printer, but that's it… you have to **DO.**

The sooner you start, the sooner you'll be dancing in the piss fountain!

Be Nice.

You might not want to do anything for anyone else for the right reasons, but if I give you a few wrong reasons, will you do the right thing anyway?

"Negative encounters feel five times more important than positive ones." – *Dr. Jeremy Sherman, Ph.D*

During an episode of one of those cooking programs, they said if you have a good experience in a restaurant you will tell four to five friends but if you have a bad one you will tell 27! Now, I could have my numbers off a bit, but you get the point. Be nice, be good. Try the fish.

People remember unexpected niceness.

If you are nice to someone that there isn't a reason for you to be nice to, your action will be surprising, unexpected and, it won't cost the earth. Maybe you're offering just a little support, a smile, or a sandwich. Your simple act of nicety won't be weighed down by undercurrents of motivations (for you to hide or the recipient to ponder on). It's pure and simple no reason nice-ness! Ahhh, isn't that lovely? Don't you feel warm and fuzzy?

Being nice actually pays off.

Anyone that is prepared to sell "help" is going to negotiate the fuck out of you (they have the help, you need the help). So, the **ONLY** way the financial equation works is from a 'buy low – sell high' perspective.

It only takes 22 muscles to smile. It takes many, many more to hit someone with a baseball bat!

New rule: be nicest to the people that there is the least reason to be nice to.

Auditioning singers...

If you are auditioning singers for your band and plan on going on the road and 'making it' here is my advice...

As the singer enters the room, listen for a while to the anecdotes of days gone by or days yet to come. Marvel as he or she weaves a tapestry of brilliant threads, joining words that were never before joined into songs that were never before sung. Look at the words as they appear to sparkle and dance in front of your eyes, and then punch the singer in the throat. I don't mean really hard, not as hard as you might want to knee him in the nuts, but, hard enough.

WHY? (At least some of you are asking.)

One simple thing you can do to move further faster is to perform 7 days a week instead of 4 or 5. It's the easiest way to make more of the difficult and real equations work. In fact, if you are a band gigging to 100 to 150 people on an o.k. night, then allowing for some extra t-shirt sales and a few more CDs over the course of 40 weeks of gigging the difference between four and seven shows a week will put an extra 75k in your pocket. $75 k.o.k.!!

You need someone fronting your band who can sing 7 shows a week, hit a few acoustic afternoon shows, and do 10 interviews a day without losing his or her voice (or at least losing it but getting it back by early morning.......).

That's my advice, punch each one in the throat. It's harsh, but fun as all hell. You have to make sure that they can deal with the throat stress that touring these days is going to rain down on them.

Branding.

Just think of branding as you being a cat, spraying all over everything, marking your territory with stinking piss....ok?

When you are creating your logo, remember this; you might need to brand something on very short notice (a tent, a person, a vehicle, a poster, a shirt, anything!)

So, the design problem here is not who can create the most complicated logo using three different techniques and hot foil printing (that takes two weeks to get back from the printer).
The design problem here is creating something that resonates with the vibe of your band and is easy to piss up a wall.

Replicate, Decorate and Communicate.
Gardening Not Architecture's logo is a mind-jogging arrangement of stenciled letters. This means that, if/when....sorry, when Sarah Saturday runs out of shirts; she can make some in the car park.

When she gets a tent to put some merchandise in at Warped tour she can stencil her name on it and **BANG,** it's hers. She owns that space. By using the logo on her CDs, she is legitimizing the D.I.Y. logo (or in her case E.I.Y. Look it up on the web).

DITTO for One Eyed Doll whose first shirts were the band's name written in bleach with a Q-Tip. **Keep it simple!**

* FROM PAGE 17
There is a contradiction here and I don't want to ignore it. One the one hand I am telling you to do as much research – due diligence, scratching below the surface as possible BUT – on the other hand I am quoting the guy from the Pabst Theater in Milwaukee who says that sometimes you have to jump off the high board before the pool has been filled with water………

Let me try and explain without bringing in the word **FUCK** (oh shit!) I'm saying that whenever you can – you **HAVE** to look at all of the available information but along the way, you'll gradually tune up your own instrument – your internal barometer of good or bad – the long forgotten instincts that make us want to fight or flee, puke or pee. The right decision for **YOU** lies somewhere in the middle of all of that. So, pay attention and (unless you are on medication) listen to those voices in your head, look at the information and, when you think it is right, **JUMP.**

Be happy with what you do!

It's the **JOY** shining out from inside of you that magnetizes people to you. When you are doing something that doesn't make you happy, how can you possibly expect it to appeal to anyone else? It won't! If this isn't what you want to do, then for fuck's sake, stop. Please, look for the thing that's **IT** for you.

Lots of people say 'you have to be passionate about the things you do' ….thats not it for me, its being **CURIOUS** - thats what keeps me noodling around experimenting with music, sounds, art, China, education, scratch and sniff 7" sleeves, flys on suits, any and all of it intrigues me - puts me in that place where you come up for air and 5 or 6 hours have gone by.

THINK about the place that does that for you - the time-eating place **- go there!**

Martin Atkins

IF you could warn someone about **ONE** thing in the music business (or life really) thats going to **FUCK THEM UP**....what would it be? and, by submitting you are agreeing to let me put it in my new book - ok?? **GO**

Jenny Adkins Henkel doubt

Lollardy Sharp Dyslexic Killing Joke.

Alain Dave Carranza Don't trust people who go out of their way in saying or acting like they are your friend. Every time I meet a really "overly nice" person they always have other motives.

Shawn Kellner The only people that really give a shit about your band is the key members and the team you put together. If members of the team you put together start to not give a shit about your band....fire them....

Thaddaeus Maximus D.J. Th@d Someone less talented than you will more than likely do better than you are. It's almost always about who you know and not what you know!

Niall Woods Other people. (I can't wait for the new book!)

Betty Machette DRUGS!

Ross Rylance Double check the background info on who your going to work for? Do they pay their bills and employees?

Patrick Swift It may just be me, but it seems to me that the first thing that fucks everyone up . . . the part where you have to grow up and decide if this is really for you, is exactly how hard you have to work, and how many things you have to get good …at or fail miserably.

I think that's where the disconnect is and where so many bands flame out and give up. You won't be a millionaire, you won't be famous, it's not going to happen for you like it did for Radiohead or Guns 'n' Roses or whoever, but you still have to spend damn near every waking moment pouring all your time, energy, and money into your band - all for the love of the music and the (often vain) hope that you can amass enough people to care about you to make it all worth it. Best of luck, kids.

Steven F Wymer fucked up shit

Nicole Rudat Be prepared for everything!

Robert Shea be responsible to know who to trust and how to deal with all the others.

Rich Denhart not following through. if you can't do that you're dead meat.

Paul Alexander Don't plan on making any money if you're in a band in limbo. Too weird, crazy, and antisocial, for the hip kids and pop scene and not weird, crazy, and antisocial enough for the experimental scene. If you're band mixes it up and hops genres too much in one song people think it's fun and that's it. Like some kind of novelty. They don't take it serious for some reason and the band fails to get recognition thus making no money. At least that's my experience from the last 12 years haha!

Brian Morphis Just enjoy it whether it's 15 minutes or a legacy, it's a whole lot better than shoveling shit.

Jonn Chapman I agree with Lol, Killing Joke have seriously fucked me up.

Phoenix Marie Paris When they try to convince you that the path to stardom involves a shared haircut, suit, and coordinated dance moves, don't listen to them!

Clifford T. Molestrangler Keep away from ham sandwiches, driving minis too fast round bends, and getting in small planes in a storm with people who call themselves things like "The Big Bopper".

Shane Bugbee credit… as in not getting paid up front. unless you're dad owns a bank you shouldn't act like one. once you give the art it can seldom be taken back so you need to get and trust is harder to find than gold.

Shane Bugbee and if you use it in the book I want credit… as in, getting credit for what I've given.

Tim Halle The one thing in the music business that people fuck up is not running their operation like a business from square 1.

Shad Foust Yep, stay off the dope, there's a reason it's called that.

Chris Motley Anything your AR person tells you is a lie.

Tony O'Reilly That it is more business than music or remember 1 day it will all come crashing down all round you also be good to your fans they buy your records & merch.

David Nicholas Add some breadth the depth of your perspective. Look sideways once in awhile instead of straight down.

Laura Ewen I agree completely with Tim Halle. It is a business after all. If you gain any sort of fame, success or credibility you MUST own your own work and have the control of it. Time and again I see so many wonderfully talented people give in to the "life" and allow the wrong, albeit charismatic people to gain too much control or access to the material that broke through. Most people are self-serving and use other's talents to their own gain.

Jeneveve Sutton Be prepared. Equipment backup. And no excuses unless it's true & crazy funny…

John Green People with big plans are usually well meaning dreamers, even if they appear to have the means to make the big plans happen. It is the people who make one little plan at a time and work hard that see those plans happen.

When somebody offers y…ou a gig, get it in writing or it is only talk.

Every band has a Yoko.

Lawrence G. Peterson Everything in moderation …

Alex Livadas Two words: disingenuous douchebags.

Thomas Papanicholas The need to separate music from business comes to mind. Really, the biz end seems to overshadow the reason to make music in the first place. Kids pick up a guitar & think they can rule the world. Meanwhile, the stodgy suits mull over how they can exploit them. Ideas become lost. The kid becomes a cog in the machine. Profits are made by the biz. & the public consume it like Lemmings. D.I.Y. is always a good rule to teach. At the very least, the ideals will (should) remain. My two cents…

Lawrence G. Peterson Just watch "Behind The Music" on VH1 and you will learn LOTS of what NOT to do. It seems like corporate types that don't know squat about music tend to screw artists up a lot! Or read Eric Burden's autobiography…

Tim Halle Here's another one. Learn how to properly operate and maintain your equipment.
Amp users: Figure out the sound you want then put together a rig accordingly and learn how to dial it in properly. I have had many bands try to get a death metal… sound with a tele and a vox or try to get a "beatles" tone out of a hopped up esp and a soldano. Not everyone has the money to get the complete rig when starting off, but you can get pretty close.
Drummers: regularly tighten and lubricate the components of your kit, and learn how to tune it properly. Even if you cant afford a top of the line kit, a well maintained cheap kit is going to sound better than a poorly maintained expensive kit.
The end result of all of this is that you will:
Sound closer to the sound that's in your head
Have faster sound checks
Spend less time in the studio looking for "the sound"

Carlos Bocanegra Be confident in your artistic vision but be aware of your deficiencies. Great albums are made with a team of creative people. Not everyone is Prince… and even he's made shitty albums.

Bill Bertrand Never trust "The Man". He got that way because of stepping on other people's necks. Always remember who you are. Live in the moment. Work for the future-live in the moment. Don't make things more complicated than they already are.

Justin Hunt get it in writing. a persons word means nothing.

Markie Sav Lojko musicians….drag u down to there level…to many hash heads, try… ing..to be nice

Juanita Brown Don't marry a band mate unless you want to make life difficult

Matt IceBreaker LaCour Friends can become different people in the studio. Keep your guard up and keep professional.

Martin Glover The first professional roadie replied when i asked him at 17 years old "what its all about?", "its not the drugs that get them and its not the money, its the women that get them in the end." tie yourself to the mast and Beware the sirens so… The Artist's journey is a long and hard quest, it's an old and ancient tradition ,no timewasters, no breadheads…read joseph Cambell 'the hero with a thousand faces" and Ullysys and "fucked by rock" by mark manning aka Zodiac Mindwarp.
Exploit the industry or it will exploit you.
Lets be honest …we are all prostitutes.
and its good to remember whether someone sits behind a desk or straddles a guitar they are still a human being and this game is all about relationships, build bridges don't burn them.
and most importantly remember a good sense of humour goes a long way.

Geoff Smyth The assumption that others will take care of things.

Carmen Stone Small venues making bands pre-sell tickets to play local shows. DIY.

Mor-Ríoghain Siobhán Mcauley
fnd the joy in every moment you can, even at 3am loading your gear back into the rehersal space in a snowstorm after 4 people showed at the gig (at least you are

following your heART) - cuz there will come moments where you think you can't t...ake one more second of everything and the only way to get through that moment is the reserve inside - be true to yourself and spend YOUR time on the earth as much in the moment as possible - be there for other people without compromising yourself and they will be there for you, or someone else will and if not at least you can look yourself in the mirror: - it ain't gonna be easy but it will be worth it in the long run and try to avoid stepping in the shit along the way

Zev Escriva Stop being a "fan" and become "the artist"
Always remain humble, always.
Help everyone who helps you and fuck those people who harm you or get in your way in any form. No second chances.
It is a job but don't ever become jaded or loose heart .. if you are not writing from your heart... You are should be writing for someone else. Or quit wasting everyones time.

Lauren Milligan When it comes to relationships, look for a significant other who already has a life - not someone who will be completely dependent on you for their happiness. There's only so long that person will want to go to your rehearsals and shows and when that's no longer satisfying, they'll pressure you to spend less time with your band, and then the real trouble starts. (Coming from a musician's wife with 16+ years of experience!)

Mercy Victor
First of all, when you are chosen by love and circumstance, talent and imagination to be an artists/musician inventor etc...You/me/us have to heed the call. Otherwise you are destined to become an empty bitter shell. And that probably fuck...ing sucks. It won't be easy. The path to being real is cluttered with the dead and dying souls of those who have tried before you. You may stop and help a few up. They may be good allies or they may fuck you up. But please try not to step on them. And most of all, you have to try and find a way to weave your dreams into your reality. You may still end up pissed off. But you will not be an empty shell. Maybe a time bomb.

Anyway, in regards to the music: Remember that the music industry is just that. A business. Maybe its a tool. Maybe not the tool you need. Whatever. Take your chances or don't, just decide if you are going to be an artist till death. Once you cross that line, whatever you do makes sense to the craft, because music is not a business. It is magic. It moves you and guides you like DNA. It is in the molecules/atoms/quarks that glue us all together so we don't fall apart. It inspires you and drives you mad. It is the human spirit bonded to song. It is the soundtrack to your/my/our life...And the fun part is, you can write your own preludes and fugues and everything in-between. BUT...remember once the desire to cross over from simply sharing to selling manifest itself (and usually it does early on) you must deal with forces that are akin to the dark side and they will by their vampiric nature try and suck out your desire to create. They need those juices to survive. Snakes will be snakes. Rats will be rats. They bite. They eat their own. They look cool. Whatever. Just be careful. Remember why and who you are. The truth/music hurts and the truth/music will set you free. Remember whats important. Ð Now go make art! My inner yoda says " the love for truth and the

love for fame/ fortune a union do not make. a great disturbance in this future. the future soul of music . clouded. in jeopardy . hmmmmm" mercy
Randall Lewis Assume.
Humboldt Lagoon A #1= drugs & booze. another might be defining your "sound" and not letting it define itself. un-originality.
Justin Nale It's a hard choice to make between dropping it all and living for your music or just having a hobby. There's advantages on both sides that you just can't get from the other. Remember the choice you've made and when hard decisions come up, stick to your choice, whichever it may be.
Zebulun Barnow The most profound repeated mistake is the belief that people, in general, are inherently "good." Business is business and it has winners and losers. Some people will win at any cost and some people just hate to lose, or they hate being losers. Part of the solution is to be prepared to be undermined by the varied intentions of others. Read "Art of War" by Sun Tzu and "Pimp" by Iceberg Slim.
Mercy Victor YES! the art of war. know the odds. choose your battles. survive to fight another day. know your enemy. and know yourself. choose your death.
"today is a good day to die"- Tasunka Witko
Martin Atkins oh thats terrific - we're really going to sell some books with CHOOSE YOUR DEATH!!! actually this is brilliant - thanks!!!
Robert Cronberg At a certain point you have to stop playing Hamlet and decide to go for it...
MisterJay Em When you borrow money from someone to do your project, you are giving that person control over you and your project. There's no such thing as no-strings-attached borrowing.
Jim Semonik If you are successful, be prepared to see other people try to take you down, steal what you have made for yourself or rip your methods off.
Robert Cronberg Not keeping a sense of groundedness and calm about you - If you can you'll be able to access inner truth, wisdom and guidance...
MisterJay Em Oral contracts are to binding agreements as oral sex is to reproduction.
Paul Whitrow Preproduction and attention to detail, don't be afraid to do what's best for the recording. Give yourself to the spiritual and imbue that energy within your work. Then it will touch others, and they won't know why...
Josh Tweedy Don't expect a music or business degree to land you a job in music. That comes from more persistence, dedication, and usually more courageous risks than the person beside you.
MisterJay Em Remember: Recreational drug use can affect your short-term...
Brice Henninger Your bill collectors don't except payment based on good intentions, so understand how finances work and earn a good living based on them.
Richard Whittaker Just because he's your mate, doesn't mean he should be your manager, and vice versa.
Johnny Angel Wendell Anything you could do yourself that you just farmed out to someone else is going to cost you a lot more than the actual service was worth.
Natalie Godstar Hendrix Tune out the bullshit. Tune in to ~you.
AND: Never, ever, ever, EVER, give up!.

Shad Foust And don't try to fit into any specific genre or category. The moment you try and be something you're not is when it all falls apart. True to yourself and your sound and all that

Arana DeeCee make sure everyone is on the same page before partnering up with anyone and leave room for compromise.

Amanda Anderson It doesn't matter how long you've known someone or how close you are with them….if its holding your band, production company, merch company, whatever…back, let them go if you're serious about what you are trying to do.

Joseph Dean Perry Addiction. Of any sort. Let it be drugs or the feeling the crowd/fans give you and get caught up in your ego

Joseph Dean Perry Stay simple minded and sober. Easier said than done right?

Chris Cozort Prepare to give much more than you will ever receive.

Mick Shearman Promote the shit out of it, work hard, have FUN!!! and get the fuck out of bed…. ;)

Kevin Scott never do what you feel is wrong and dont be pushed into something that you do not want to do. BE YOURSELF, ALWAY'S.

Carson Duke McClain Ð"Wanting" to become a world famous audio engineer does not mean you should be. Borrowing tens of thousands of dollars to go to audio school does not make you an audio engineer. Buy your own gear, spend every waking moment using it and plan on doing a lot of work initially for free. If you're not willing to do this, you should find another profession.

Luke Stokes do not sign your merch rights over. the difference is could be a .50 cents a shirt sold vs. $14.00 or more a shirt sold.

If your thinking they can can get you into to hot topic does it really even make sense unless you know your selling unit…s through hot topic. i could go on and on here about this one.

Kevin Sullivan NEVER PLUG YOUR GEAR DIRECTLY INTO A VENUE OUTLET! Or any outlet for that matter. Always use a surge protector, and a nice one like Monster Cable brand, not some cheap piece of junk from the dollar store. $80+ might seem like a lot at the …time but never having tor stop mid-set because your $3000 Amplifier/Keyboard/PA or whatever is completely fried is well worth the money.

Also have an emergency box with things like a soldering iron, duct and electrical tape, 9v batteries, extra power supplies, sharpies, a multi-tool, wirecutters, screwdrivers, extra strings and cables, a copy of Tour Smart, etc… anything that can go wrong will at some point and you want to be prepared for it.

Jane Jensen

Once you start having some success there is heavy pressure to upgrade your "team" ie, band members, manager, etc.

once you start severing relationships in the music business, I think you can expect it to come back around to you…

Everyone w…ill say that so and so is a lying, stealing, dirt bag. That may or may not be true but everyone will say that about everyone else- these are the people you learn to work with. Don't sever relationships until you are sure you have a better place to be…..a little less lying, stealing and dirt baggyness, for example.

Also, if you're female, take a vow of chastity and don't have sex until after you have reached your career goals.

Paul Wendell Obis Don't take it personally it's just blood and tears.

Shaun Buehler Accentuate the positive, eliminate the negative :)

Robbie Ballentine BAD INFORMATION ! Check it, check it again & then when you think it's accurate, check it again and again!

Dan Milligan You will eventually have to fire a good friend.

Krztoff Bile Don't work with Martin Atkins, he's fucking crazy.

Ha! I couldn't help it.

Aaron McCall prepare for the worst.. something will break, bend or blow up. You cant stop it but you can prepare your self to deal with it and roll on with out effecting your progress too much

Bari Davis No matter how good an artist one is, charisma when used properly will get you what you want over talent everytime.

Heidi Epling be nice. be honest. be kind.

don't give a (*#$&) about what you think other people want. do what you love.

Christopher Hall every person in the industry wants a percentage of you and everyone of those people have 10 friends who also want a percentage of you. the entire industry is designed to suck every penny earned from your music. every time someone offers to …help it comes with a price and although 5% here and 10% there may not seem like a big deal it all adds up. the guy tuning your guitar while you are playing on stage to thousands will end up with a house in tahoe while you make your girlfriend strip an extra shift to pay the rent on your N hollywood apt. your manager drives a mercedes while you eat ramen. your agent doesn't care that you wasted $300 in gas because of bad routing. he still get's his 15%. so either DIY or enjoy the memories. because that's all you will have in the end.

Christopher Hall if someone tells you to do something that you feel is a bad idea DON"T DO IT! just try on this stupid fucking red suit for one picture if you don't like it we won't use it. But they WILL use it. just sing it once like this if you don't lik…e it we don't have to use it. they WILL use it. if you don't want it out there don't do it. no matter what pressure they put on you. you have to live with yourself and your fans for the rest of your now greatly shortened career. they will just find another schmuck to exploit and destroy.

Carson Duke McClain Doing what you love may not always make you money. Doing what other people love will always make you money. DJ's and Cover bands are more popular than ever.

Sid Sickness if you find that some one is bootlegging your material, like demos/live shows, take a step back and think 'wow, now thats a fan!' these fanatics go to GREAT lengths to create these things, b/c they are the uberfans, remember that! THEN consider suing the bastard! (then proceed to explain how its done in this day and age where yr show gets put on youtube the next day)

Billy Ludwig Don't burn bridges,.. it could come back to haunt you. I've always found it amusing (and annoying) one someone (band, musician, venue etc.etc.) has been disrespectful in the past, and then comes back later on needing my "help"

Robert Cronberg Never get too high....Never get too low.... you'll experience both frequently....

Andrew Lasswell Remove your lip stitches before getting in the rubber dinghy!

Ada Ruiz the music industry is like a fast food chain, the turn around is atrocious. if you hang in there, for long enough, you'll be making the fries. but right when you start making fries, they are going to want onion rings.

Wes Imel Appreciate all comments.. Even the negative ones.. The biggest insult you can give an artist is to have no opinion at all.

Wes Imel Best piece of advice I can give a musician right here:
Go to a bookstore and buy TOUR SMART: And Break the Band by Martin Atkins.

Harpo Mark Delguidice never sign anything you dont understand..and READ steve albini,s article; `so you wanna sign a record deal huh?` before you do ..seriously

Scott Parker Don't become the "Be All, End All", the latter is soon to occur.

Amanda Anderson if you are in a situation where you HAVE to work with/for someone who is known to use/take advantage of others, make sure that you get something out of it even if they don't realise that they're giving it to you. sometimes the worst examples are the best ones to learn from. (just ask me about my first touring experience...haha)

Nora Hayes Eldredge Don't ever sell your music publishing rights.

Mark Spybey Do not mix peanut butter, rye bread and salsa together in front of someone from Arizona.

Kadin Contois fuck the middleman.

Milinda F Grant for get the manager.....dont need one-promote yourselfs;)

Nicole Spaulding Music IS Who You Are, Not Just What You Do.

Alisa Yates 1) marriage within bands tends to be disasterous. 2)and if you're really really really talented, you should definitely not let your mate discourage you from pursuing a musical career

Alisa Yates oh and a really really big one for me, is take time to appreciate your supporters (fans) i actually like some bands much more than others just because they were nicer to me and took the time out to appreciate their other fans as well

Stan Sikorski Don't sign anything over to the company/producer.

Mick Robert Cetera excuses

Shannon Gausten The days of the multi-million dollar making garage band are over. Don't plan on making any money on sales of your music. Illegal downloaders don't give a shit about you and the fact that you need the revenue to continue to afford to make a product. 'Cause you know, its just a "copy" its not like STEALING or anything, because showing your respect for someone's output by purchasing it is soooo 1999.

Oedipus Oedipus Don't sue your fans or let anyone sue them in your name. Give as much as you can (including your music) and they will give back to you in kind.

Naive Quiet Ask them to reconsider their dreams which were not fully thought out in the begining. Or that's what got 'us' this far!?

SOLUBLE BOOKS
ISBN 978-9-780-97973-7 51499
13100 >

blurb.com